The Mind-Body Problem

KATHA POLLITT

The Mind-Body Problem

Poems

RANDOM HOUSE | NEW YORK

Published in the United States by Random House,
an imprint of The Random House Publishing Group,
a division of Random House, Inc., New York.

RANDOM HOUSE and colophon are registered
trademarks of Random House, Inc.

Original publication information for some
of the poems in this collection
can be found on pages 81–82.

LIBRARY OF CONGRESS CATALOGING-IN-PUBLICATION DATA
Pollitt, Katha.
The mind-body problem: poems / Katha Pollitt.
p. cm.
ISBN 978-1-4000-6333-8
I. Title.
PS3566.0533M56 2009
811'.54—dc22   2008037986

Printed in the United States of America on acid-free paper

www.atrandom.com

2 4 6 8 9 7 5 3 1

FIRST EDITION

Book design by Rebecca Aidlin

For Sophie
and
for Steven

CONTENTS

I

The Mind-Body Problem

Mind-Body Problem / 3

Lives of the Nineteenth-Century Poetesses / 5

A Walk / 6

Aere Perennius / 7

Collectibles / 8

Signs and Portents / 10

Shore Road / 12

Integer Vitae / 14

Lilacs in September / 15

Mandarin Oranges / 16

Playground / 17

Rereading Jane Austen's Novels / 19

Atlantis / 20

Abandoned Poems / 22

Visitors / 23

A Chinese Bowl / 25

Amor Fati / 28

Milkweed / 29

Night Subway / 30

II

After the Bible

The Expulsion / 33

Cities of the Plain / 35

Lot's Wife / 36

In the Bulrushes / 37

Job / 39

Moth / 40

Martha / 42

The Cursed Fig Tree / 44

Rapture / 45

III

Lunaria

Happiness Writes White / 49

From a Notebook / 50

Maya / 51

Old Sonnets / 53

Epithalamion / 54

Two Cats / 56

Near Union Square / 58

The Old Neighbors / 59

The Heron in the Marsh / 61

Forwarding Address / 62

What I Understood / 64

Evening in the Mugello / 65

Always Already / 66

Walking in the Mist / 67

The White Room / 69

Trying to Write a Poem Against the War / 70

Old / 71

Silent Letter / 72

Dreaming About the Dead / 73

Small Comfort / 75

Wisdom of the Desert Fathers / 76

Lunaria / 78

Acknowledgments / 81

I. The Mind-Body Problem

Mind-Body Problem

When I think of my youth I feel sorry not for myself
but for my body. It was so direct
and simple, so rational in its desires,
wanting to be touched the way an otter
loves water, the way a giraffe
wants to amble the edge of the forest, nuzzling
the tender leaves at the tops of the trees. It seems
unfair, somehow, that my body had to suffer
because I, by which I mean my mind, was saddled
with certain unfortunate high-minded romantic notions
that made me tyrannize and patronize it
like a cruel medieval baron, or an ambitious
English-professor husband ashamed of his wife—
her love of sad movies, her budget casseroles
and regional vowels. Perhaps
my body would have liked to make some of our dates,
to come home at four in the morning and answer my scowl
with "None of your business!" Perhaps
it would have liked more presents: silks, mascaras.
If we had had a more democratic arrangement
we might even have come, despite our different backgrounds,
to a grudging respect for each other, like Tony Curtis
and Sidney Poitier fleeing handcuffed together,
instead of the current curious shift of power

in which I find I am being reluctantly
dragged along by my body as though by some
swift and powerful dog. How eagerly
it plunges ahead, not stopping for anything,
as though it knows exactly where we are going.

Lives of the Nineteenth-Century Poetesses

As girls they were awkward and peculiar,
wept in church or refused to go at all.
Their mothers saw right away no man would marry them.
So they must live at the sufferance of others,
timid and queer as governesses out of Chekhov,
malnourished on theology, boiled eggs, and tea,
but given to outbursts of pride that embarrass everyone.
After the final quarrel, the grand
renunciation, they retire upstairs to the attic
or to the small room in the cheap off-season hotel
and write *Today I burned all your letters* or
I dreamed the magnolia blazed like an avenging angel
and when I woke I knew I was in Hell.
No one is surprised when they die young,
having left all their savings to a wastrel nephew,
to be remembered for a handful
of "minor but perfect" lyrics,
a passion for jam or charades,
and a letter still preserved in the family archives:
"I send you herewith the papers of your aunt
who died last Tuesday in the odor of sanctity
although a little troubled in her mind
by her habit, much disapproved of by the ignorant,
of writing down the secrets of her heart."

A Walk

When I go for a walk and see they're tearing down
some old red-plush Rialto for an office building
and suddenly realize this was where Mama and I
saw *Lovers of Teruel* three times in a single sitting

and the drugstore where we went afterward for ice cream's
gone, too, and Mama's gone and my ten-year-old self,
I admire more than ever the ancient Chinese poets
who were comforted in exile by thoughts of the transience
    of life.

How *yesterday,* for instance, *quince bloomed in the emperor's*
    courtyard
but today wild geese fly south over ruined towers.
Or, *Oh, full moon that shone on our scholarly wine parties,*
do you see us now, scattered on distant shores?

A melancholy restraint is surely the proper approach
to take in this world. And so I walk on, recall-
ing Hsin Ch'i-chi, who when old and full of sadness
wrote merely, *A cool day, a fine fall.*

Aere Perennius

The mugger leaping out with his quick knife,
the waitress who does porno on the side,
even the stray dog, methodically marking

the acidulated saplings one by one—
what are they but life insisting on its life,
its own small heat, *Don't let me pass away*

with nothing to show for it, as the wind passes
over the grass as though it had never been?
Clouds give birth to themselves in the windy sky

over and over, last year's leaves lie
quiet under last year's snow. That we're not these
nor would be if we could is our whole meaning:

marble, murder, saxophones, lipstick, Nero
wasting the empire for the Golden House
in which he could live, at last, "like a human being."

Collectibles

Even jumbled here in the schoolyard rummage sale
they keep their spirits up. This battered tin
combination cheese-and-nutmeg shaver
still offers *"Gratings" from Fort Lauderdale,*
this bunch of velvet violets breathes a pale,
still-shocking scent of lingerie, and here
(but where's your mate? Your shiny silver cap?)
is—can it be?—the purple jug-shaped blown-
glass salt shaker from my parents' breakfast table.
A manic friendliness infuses these
things that mostly look like other things—
the tomato that holds thread, the black-and-white
kitten teapot, one paw raised for spout—
like toys that in a child's dream play all night
or like the magic kitchens in cartoons
where pots and pans leap down from the shelf and dance
and the orange squeezer oompahs like a tuba.
Innocent, foolish, jaunty, trivial,
small travelers from a land that thought it was
so full of love and coziness and cheer

the least things shared in it—why should
they pain us so somehow, who know so well
it wasn't like that, not really, even then?
Is that what they have come so far to tell us?
That we lose even what we never had?

Signs and Portents

Only natural, to put
a face on the world: the little
cousins deep in the big
four-poster, giggling, *Ooh*

*look, cats peeking
through the wallpaper squiggles!* And
consider the letdown, despite
the scallion pancakes, the shrimp

garnished with walnuts and pungent
assassinations of character,
the oranges sliced and prinked
into petals, to unfold

some fake Confucian proverb
and not, *For you, pink-
faced barbarian, gold,
palm trees, perversions!* No

wonder herdsmen squinting
at the stars through sheep-dung smoke,
giddy with beer, kif, boredom,
nudged each other: a spoon!

a xylophone! a breast! So that
this morning Mrs. Holmquist
opens the paper and feels
Aquarius unmistakably

bend to her ear: *My child,*
new lawsuits mean new hairstyles.
Who wants to know what we know?
The bush in the desert aflame

because of a flung cigarette,
the pigeons swooping the Forum
only for bread crumbs, the loved
voice on the answering machine

revealing no note of personal
interest previously lacking
and the message always the same:
I am not here. I will

not return your call.

Shore Road

Amazing how they hang on,
these battered bungalows
with jaunty names from the forties—
Mairzy Doats, On The Rocks, At-Eze,

Shipshape, its upstairs prow
sagging like the toe of an ancient
upside-down boot.
The porch swings are peeling,

the children have their own lives.
Still, somebody
crew-cuts the crab grass
that ends in beach or marsh,

puts out the plastic lawn chairs,
launders the white curtains.
Through which one glimpses
bedrooms that glow pale yellow

or lilac, like Easter eggs.
On the dresser, Mass cards, seashells,
photos—Sue and the girls
and what was his name? The dog

who loved chocolate ice cream?
Terrible how you forget, but
never mind, it's another morning
for the Kerrys and Angelinis

hoisting their Irish and Italian flags
as if it didn't matter that they're going,
like the geese unraveling
southward over the sea grass,

a few less every year,
like "swell" and "swank"
or the girls' names on the housefronts:
Miss New Britain. Wendy-Ann.

Integer Vitae

The beautiful gray dog
loping across the lawn
all afternoon for the sheer
joy of summertime,

bees at their balm, the dragonfly
asleep on a raspberry leaf—
that's how we'd live
if living were enough:

innocent, single-hearted
like the mourning dove who's called
his mate in the cool dawn
from one pine for a thousand years.

These do not wake in tears
nor does deception drive them
down to the blue pond
where the beaver, prince

of chaos, who appeared
alone as if from nowhere,
is tirelessly constructing
his dark palace of many rooms.

Lilacs in September

Shocked to the root
like the lilac bush
in the vacant lot
by the hurricane—

whose black branch split
by wind or rain
has broken out
unseasonably

into these scant ash-
colored blossoms
lifted high
as if to say

to passersby
What will unleash
itself in you
when your storm comes?

Mandarin Oranges

I can't remember if I even liked them
when they were the special treat of our high-school lunchroom.
Probably not—they smacked of bribery:

for chapel, volleyball, and lima beans,
this splash of the Orient in a thin sugary plasma.
And yet today at the supermarket I

Saw that silly geisha flirt her fan
against the flat, insipid turquoise sea
and wanted mandarin oranges more than

I've ever wanted anything, as if
they held the whole essence of youth and joy. O sweetness,
sunrise, hibiscus, Chinese lanterns, hearts—

we can't keep faith with the past,
in the end we love it because it is the past,
no matter how stubbornly we tell ourselves,

"Remember what this was like,
how bored you were, how miserable." Inscribed
in a margin of *Modern Chemistry* and dated
March 15, 1965.

Playground

In the hygienic sand
of the new municipal sandbox,
children with names from the soaps,
Brandon and Samantha,
fill and empty, fill and empty
their bright plastic buckets
alongside children with names
from obscure books of the Bible.
We are all mothers here,
friendly and polite.
We are teaching our children to share.

A man could slice his way
through us like a pirate!
And why not? Didn't we open
our bodies recklessly
to any star, say, Little one,
whoever you are, come in?
But the men are busy elsewhere.
Broad-hipped in fashionable sweatpants,
we discuss the day—a tabloid
murder, does cold cream work,
those students in China—

and as we talk
not one of us isn't thinking
Mama! Was it like this?
Did I do this to you?
But Mama too is busy,
she is dead, or in Florida,
or taking up new interests,
and the children want apple juice
and Cheerios, diapers and naps.
We have no one to ask but each other.
But we do not ask each other.

Rereading Jane Austen's Novels

This time round, they didn't seem so comic.
Mama is foolish, dim or dead, Papa's
a sort of genial, pampered lunatic.
No one thinks of anything but class.

Talk about rural idiocy! Imagine
a life of tea with Mrs. and Miss Bates,
of fancy work and Mr. Elton's sermons!
No wonder lively girls get into states—

no school, no friends. A man might dash to town
just to have his hair cut in the fashion
while she can't walk five miles on her own.
Past twenty, she conceives a modest crush on

some local stuffed shirt in a riding cloak
who's twice her age and maybe half as bright.
At least he's got some land and gets a joke—
but will her jokes survive the wedding night?

The happy end ends all. Beneath the blotter
the author slides her page, and shakes her head,
and goes to supper—Sunday's joint warmed over,
followed by whist, and family prayers, and bed.

Atlantis

Dreaming of our golden boulevards and temples,
our painted palaces set in torchlit gardens,
our spires and minarets, our emerald harbor,
you won't want to hear about the city we knew:

the narrow neighborhoods of low white houses
where workmen come home for lunch and an afternoon nap,
old women in sweat-stained penitential black
ease their backaches gratefully against doorways

and the widow who keeps the corner grocery
anxiously watches her child dragging his toy
who was sickly from birth and everyone knows must die soon.
You won't want to know how we lived,

the hot sun, the horse traders cheating each other out of
    boredom,
in the brothels the prostitutes curling each other's hair
while the madam limps upstairs to feed the canary,
the young louts smoking in bare cafés

where old men play dominoes for glasses of cognac—
and how can we blame you?
We too were in love with something we never could name.
We never could let ourselves say

that the way the harbor flashed like bronze at sunset
or the hill towns swam in the twilight like green stars
were only tricks of the light and meant nothing.
We too believed that a moment would surely come

when our lives would stand hard and pure, like marble statues.
And because we were, after all, only a poor city,
a city like others, of sailors' bars and sunflowers,
we gave ourselves up to be only a name,

an image of temples and spires and jeweled gardens
for which reasons we are envied of all peoples,
and even now could not say
what life would have to be, for us to have chosen it.

Abandoned Poems

It's awful how they look at you: consumptive,
all eyes in their white beds,
coughing delicately into their handkerchiefs
and feebly hissing, *Don't leave us here, you bastard,*
this is your fault. What can you do but agree?
It's no use to harden your heart,
no use to explain why you had to save yourself,
still less to confess how happy you are without them,
how already you see yourself under the trees in the park:
you read the paper, you eat a ham sandwich,
then shake out the crumbs for the pigeons
and walk on, savoring
the mild autumnal air of your new country,
the kingdom of health and silence.

Visitors

The senile bat with nicotine-streaked hair
hefting and sniffing cantaloupes at Key Food—
where had I seen before
that look, shrewd, absorbed, like a bird with a seed?

Of course. I almost cried out "Madame
Champrigand!" Who taught us girls *Topaze*
and the *belle logique* of the *pari-mutuel* system—
and there was a long pause

before I thought, *but she's been dead for years.*
This happens not infrequently—more often
too as I get older—the dead appear
not, as you might imagine,

to startle us with fear or guilt or grief
or the cold fact of our own mortality,
but just to take pleasure again in everyday life:
to walk the dog, or stand in line for a movie,

or pick up a quart of milk and the Sunday *Times.*
Why shouldn't they have an outing? All the same,
it must embarrass them to use their day-
passes in such a modest way

which is why when we glimpse them they quickly
dart round the corner or step behind a tree
or cleverly melt into strangers. Only you,
loved shade, do I never see

across the traffic or ahead in the surge of shoppers
swept off into the just-closing elevator door.
Was life so bitter, then, that even these
innocent errands cannot lure you here

for just one afternoon? I would not speak
even your name, you would not have to see me
shadow you drifting down the sunny sidewalk
happy and idle, free. And when you came

at last to the dark and silent subway stairwell
I would not cry or insist. For I would know
you finally: separate, as you were, yourself.
I would not keep you. I would let you go.

A Chinese Bowl

Plucked from a junk shop
chipped celadon
. shadow of a swallow's wing
or cast by venetian blinds

on tinted legal pads
one summer Saturday
in 1957.
Absorbed at his big desk

my father works on briefs.
The little Royal makes
its satisfying *chock*s
stamping an inky nimbus

around each thick black letter
with cut-out moons for "O"s.
Curled up on the floor,
I'm writing too: "Bean Soup

and Rice," a play about
a poor girl in Kyoto
and the treasure-finding rabbit
who saves her home. Fluorescent

light spills cleanly down
on the Danish Modern couch
and metal cabinet
which hides no folder labeled

"blacklist" or "Party business"
or " drink" or "mother's death."
I think, This is happiness,
right here, right now, these

walls striped green and gray,
shadow and sun, dust motes
stirring the still air,
and a feeling gathers, heavy

as rain about to fall,
part love, part concentration,
part inner solitude.
Where is that room, those gray-

green thin-lined
scribbled papers
littering the floor?
How did

I move so far away
just living day by day,
that now all rooms seem strange,
the years all error?
        Bowl,

what could
I drink from you,
clear green tea
or iron-bitter water

that would renew
my fallen life?

Amor Fati

Everywhere I look I see my fate.
In the subway. In a stone.
On the curb where people wait for the bus in the rain.
In a cloud. In a glass of wine.

When I go for a walk in the park it's a sycamore leaf.
At the office, a dull pencil.
In the window of Woolworth's my fate looks back at me
through the shrewd eyes of a dusty parakeet.

Scrap of newspaper, dime in a handful of change,
down what busy street do you hurry this morning,
an overcoat among overcoats,

with a train to catch, a datebook full of appointments?
If I called you by my name would you turn around
or vanish round the corner,
leaving a faint odor of orange-flower water,
tobacco, twilight, snow?

Milkweed

Ghost feathers, angel bones, I see them rise
over West Thirteenth Street, unearthly, shining,
tiny Quixotes sailing off to heaven
right on schedule: it's the end of August.
I'm tired of transcendence. Let's stay home
tonight, just us, let's take the phone off the hook
and drink a peaceable beer on the fire escape.
Across the darkening garden, our lesbian neighbor
is watering her terraceful of scraggly geraniums,
the super and his wife are having a salsa party,
and in a little while the moon will rise
over the weary municipal London plane trees
and the old classical philologist next door
will look up from his lexicon and remember
that even Zeus came down to us for love.
Love, we could do worse than listen to the city breathing
on its way to bed tonight while overhead
cold galaxies of milkweed stream and stream.

Night Subway

The nurse coming off her shift at the psychiatric ward
nodding over the *Post,* her surprisingly delicate legs
shining darkly through the white hospital stockings,
and the Puerto Rican teens, nuzzling, excited
after heavy dates in Times Square, the girl with green hair,
the Hasid from the camera store, who mumbles
over his prayerbook the nameless name of God,
sitting separate, careful no woman should touch him,
even her coat, even by accident,
the boy who squirms on his seat to look out the window
where signal lights wink and flash like the eyes of dragons
while his mother smokes, each short, furious drag
meaning *Mens no good they tell you anything—*

How not think of Xerxes, how he reviewed his troops
and wept to think that of all those thousands of men
in their brilliant armor, their spearpoints bright in the sun,
not one would be alive in a hundred years?

O sleepers above us, river
rejoicing in the moon, and the clouds passing over the moon.

II. After the Bible

The Expulsion

Adam was happy—now he had someone to blame
for everything: shipwrecks, Troy,
the gray face in the mirror.

Eve was happy—now he would always need her.
She walked on boldly, swaying her beautiful hips.

The serpent admired his emerald coat,
the Angel burst into flames
(he'd never approved of them, and he was right).

Even God was secretly pleased: Let
History begin!

The dog had no regrets, trotting by Adam's side
self-importantly, glad to be rid

of the lion, the toad, the basilisk, the white-footed mouse,
who were also happy and forgot their names immediately.

Only the Tree of Knowledge stood forlorn,
its small hard bitter crab apples

glinting high up, in a twilight of black leaves.
How pleasant it had been, how unexpected

to have been, however briefly,
the center of attention.

Cities of the Plain

After he vaporized the pleasure gardens,
the temples of Luck and Mirrors, the striped
tents of the fortune-tellers,
after he'd rained down sulphur
on the turquoise baths, the peacock market,
the street of painted boys,
obliterated the city, with all its people,
down to the last stray cat and curious stink,
he missed them. Killing them
made him want to kill them again—

how cleverly they'd escaped him,
hiding in corners and laughing,
just out of sight!

Being God, he would not permit himself regrets.
There would be other cities, just as wicked.
But none like Sodom, none like Gomorrah.
Probably he has been angry ever since—
angry and lonely.

Lot's Wife

Trudging behind the broad backside of God
she hums her useless tune
Oh little black dress at the back of the closet,
who will crush you now against his chest?

Green Italian boots in a midnight window,
a scrabble of rats, a hand
lit from within like a tulip—
Who dashes down that street to meet her lover?
Who sits in the movie theater
coiled, silent, a black cat?

The dark-eyed daughters idly stroke their breasts.
A jackal crouches in shadow, hungry for salt.
At the base of a dune that heaves to the blank horizon
a palm tree shrugs its shoulders
as if to say: Well, what did you expect?

In the Bulrushes

Lotus. Papyrus. Turquoise. Lapis. Gold.
A jackal-headed god
nods in the noon
that shimmers over the river
as if fanned by invisible slave girls.
Frogs fall silent, stunned
by the sun or eternity.
The Pyramids have been crumbling for centuries.

Snug in his bassinet of reeds
the lucky baby plays with his toes,
naked. What does he care
for his mother's eyes in a thorn tree?
Around his head an alphabet of flames
spells Thunder. Transformation.
Woe to women.

The sun begins its red plunge down the sky.
Deep in the earth a locust's eyes snap open.
Frogs resume their trill.

And punctual to the minute
down the path,
tottering on jeweled sandals, comes
the beautiful lonely princess

who's wandered in from another kind of story.

Job

Worse than the boils and sores
and the stench and the terrible flies
was the nattering: *Think.*
You must have done something.
Things happen for a reason.
What goes around.

His life swept off in a whirlwind of camels and children!
Still, he knew enough to shut up
when his skin cleared pink as a baby's
and overnight lambs blanketed the burnt fields.
People even said he looked taller
in his fine new robes: *You see?*
When one door closes, two doors open.

Nobody wanted to hear
about the rain or its father
or leviathan slicing the deeps
at the black edge of the world
under the cold blue light of the Pleiades.

The new sons were strong and didn't ask difficult questions,
the new daughters beautiful, with glass-green eyes.

Moth

Matthew 6:19

Come bumble-footed ones,
dust squigglers, furry ripplers,

inchers and squirmers
humble in gray and brown,

find out our secret places,
devour our hearts,

measure us, geometer, with your curved teeth!
Leaves lick at the window, clouds

stream away,
yet we lie here,

perfect,
locked in our dark chambers

when we could rise in you
brief, splendid

twentyplume, gold-
spotted ghost, pink scavenger,

luna whose pale green wings
glow with moons and planets

at one with the burning world,
whose one desire is to escape itself.

Martha

Well, did he think the food would cook itself?
Naturally, he preferred the sexy one,
the one who leaned forward with velvet eyes and asked

clever questions that showed she'd done the reading.
You'll notice he didn't summon up a picnic
so that I could put up my feet and hear how lilies

do nothing but shine in God's light. God's
movie star, he says
we stand in glory, we are loved like sparrows,

like grains of sand: there are so many of us!
He means he stands, he is loved.
The music wells up in the dark theater:

a kiss, a kill, a tumult of clouds and cymbals!
We lift our hands, we weep, we don't deserve him.
I don't deserve him. I'm

all wrong, I'm nothing, hurrying home
in my raincoat and practical shoes.
The sky won't speak to me. But still,

somebody's got to care about the tablecloth
and the bread, and the wine.

The Cursed Fig Tree

Before his hunger
I stood mute.
I did not flower.
I did not fruit.

My broad leaves stirred.
A bird flew over.
He shook his fist
and muttered: *Wither.*

I would have been happy
to grant his wish.
But it was April,
too soon for figs.

Is that why he cursed me?
Because he saw
in me his own
futility?

A bend in the road
and he was gone,
helpless in his world
as I in mine.

Rapture

It is just as they knew it would be:
the proof
of their rightness spread around them
like grass or sidewalks

among the bland custardy palaces
and picnic tables
of their reward. The air
smells of children and coconuts. Truth
blares from every station on the dial.

Do they miss dogs, the black
squelch of November, maples
wringing their red hands?
Are they saddened

to meet an old love without pain
in the gilded, silent grove
that lately, come to think of it,
has been looking rather dusty,
and where less and less often
        they feel someone watching?

The angels are kind, like waiters, but
    not very talkative.

No wonder they gather, like exiles
straining toward faint reports
crackling up from below—
war, disaster, stars plunging into the sea.

God, it appears, is elsewhere, even here.

III. Lunaria

Happiness Writes White

So what good is it? Let's be sad,
wear melancholy like an old brown sweater
patched at the elbows and smelling of our own funk.
The coffee cups pile up on the little table,
pages turn, electric lights come on—
it would be good to have a dog, you think,
one with grave eyes and an understanding of life,
it would be good

to go down to the docks and watch the freighters
idly listing in the oily water,
to smoke a cigarette and look out at the sea
and then walk home in the gathering evening,
at a measured pace, still hearing the voice of the sea
that speaks to you like a friend, of serious things
so simply and quietly
you barely notice the sky blanch after rain
or the woman coming out of the subway
carrying an immense bouquet of white lilac
wrapped in white tissue paper, like a torch.

From a Notebook

The final vanity, to think
you're not your life, that even today
at the last possible moment
you can walk away, as out of a cheap hotel,
leaving ten dollars under the key on the bureau.
Why bother to lock the door? The fuzzy TV,
the footsole-colored bedspread,
the quart of milk souring on the windowsill,
you always knew they had nothing to do with you
although you were used to them
and even grateful,
alone as you were, in a strange city.

Maya

for Anna Fels

It's all maya—that's what we used to say,
Zen friends forever, rushing into the dorm
flushed from our dash through the common,
        stamping our snow-
caked boots like Cossacks: all illusion, term

papers, bad sex, no sex, my antique
real-lace camisole
lifted by the class kleptomaniac
and smuggled in atonement to Goodwill—

how scornfully we flung into our bon-
fire mere phenomena, all shadows, dreams,
as though it was not we who burned, our own
vitality we watched go up in flames!

It's all maya—I still say that, Cartesian
to the end, and yet it comes back differently
now I believe it, everything is illusion
and yet is no less everything: love, safety,

the warm living room and the October sun
slant on the good rug, or the train today
from which I watched, beyond my dim reflection,
the silent, bright elms burn themselves away.

Old Sonnets

Here is a public garden hedged with iron:
a beaux-arts Psyche lifts obediently
her white stone lamp against a stone sky.
A single carp hangs gold in its blackened basin.
Who is that girl in the black sweater,
smoking and scribbling furiously?
When she looks up, you might imagine she
is trying to decipher

the passionflower-purple graffito
flung at a passing bus—*who* 101?—
or listens for the insistent radio
that prowls the damp air, nearing, fading, nearing.
But no: what makes her look so tense and drawn
is the effort of not seeing, of not hearing.

Epithalamion

The boy who scribbled *Smash the State* in icing
on his wedding cake has two kids and a co-op,
reads (although pretends not to) the Living Section
and hopes for tenure.

Everything's changed since we played Capture the Red Flag
between Harvard Yard and the river. Which of us dreamed that
History, who grinds men up like meat, would
make us its next meal?

But here we are, in a kind of post-imperial
permanent February, with offices and apartments,
balked latecomers out of a Stendhal novel,
our brave ambitions

run out into sand: into restaurants and movies,
July at the Cape, where the major source of amusement's
watching middle-aged Freudians snub only just younger
Marxist historians.

And yet if it's true, as I've read, that the starving body
eats itself, it's true too it eats the heart last.
We've lost our moment of grandeur, but come on, admit it:
aren't we happier?

And so let's welcome the child already beginning,
who'll laugh, but not cruelly, I hope, at our comfy nostalgias,
and praise, friends, praise, this marriage of friends and lovers
made in a dark time.

Two Cats

It's better to be a cat than to be a human.
Not because of their much-noted grace and beauty—
their beauty wins them no added pleasure, grace is
only a cat's way

of getting without fuss from one place to another—
but because they see things as they are. Cats never mistake a
saucer of milk for a declaration of passion
or the crook of your knees for

a permanent address. Observing two cats on a sunporch,
you might think of them as a pair of Florentine bravoes
awaiting through slitted eyes the least lapse of attention—
then slash! the stiletto

or alternately as a long-married couple, who hardly
notice each other but find it somehow a comfort
sharing the couch, the evening news, the cocoa.
Both these ideas

are wrong. Two cats together are like two strangers
cast up by different storms on the same desert island
who manage to guard, despite the utter absence
of privacy, chocolate,

useful domestic articles, reading material,
their separate solitudes. They would not dream of
telling each other their dreams, or the plots of old movies,
or inventing a bookful

of coconut recipes. Where we would long ago have
frantically shredded our underwear into signal
flags and be dancing obscenely about on the shore in
a desperate frenzy,

they merely shift on their haunches, calm as two stoics
weighing the probable odds of the soul's immortality,
as if to say, if a ship should happen along we'll
be rescued. If not, not.

Near Union Square

Hard and pure, like a pared primitive weapon
glinting with blood and black necessity,
the firelight dancing at the back of the cave
where the magic drawings are—who wouldn't want,
in theory, a life like that? But on 14th Street
the Dominican peddlers sell Windex-blue ices,
plastic shoes, and rugs on which a bulldog
is cheating two beagles and a dachshund at cards
and suddenly out of nowhere the roof of every
flaking office building flares gold as though
it was not going to be demolished tomorrow
and everyone has the same American thought:
Everything is possible. I walk on
in my new three-dollar lime-translucent sandals
content to be at home in this crumbling
city of appearances and salsa
whose rotting wharves, from a distance, smell like flowers.

The Old Neighbors

The weather's turned, and the old neighbors creep out
from their crammed rooms to blink in the sun, as if
surprised to find they've lived through another winter.
Though steam heat's left them pale and shrunken
like old root vegetables,
Mr. and Mrs. Tozzi are already
hard at work on their front-yard mini-Sicily:
a Virgin Mary birdbath, a thicket of roses,
and the only outdoor aloes in Manhattan.
It's the old immigrant story,
the beautiful babies
grown up into foreigners. Nothing's
turned out the way they planned
as sweethearts in the sinks of Palermo. Still,
each waves a dirt-caked hand
in geriatric fellowship with Stanley,
the former tattoo king of the Merchant Marine,
turning the corner with his shaggy collie,
who's hardly three but trots
arthritically in sympathy. It's only
the young who ask if life's worth living, not
Mrs. Sansanowitz, who for the last hour
has been inching her way down the sidewalk,
lifting and placing

her new aluminum walker as carefully
as a spider testing its web. On days like these,
I stand for a long time
under the wild gnarled root of the ancient wisteria,
dry twigs that in a week
will manage a feeble shower of purple blossom,
and I believe it: this is all there is,
all history's brought us here to our only life
to find, if anywhere,
our hanging gardens and our street of gold:
cracked stoops, geraniums, fire escapes, these old
stragglers basking in their bit of sun.

The Heron in the Marsh

At the end of summer
stands white and alone
a question mark

among the green reeds
that glow even as they fail.
Wanderer, lordless
samurai

with only yourself for armor,
tell me, why is loss real
even when love was not?
The tide seeps in,

the dark sand shines.
You lift your strong wings
and skim away
over the gray

and glittering
open water.

Forwarding Address

Ten blocks downtown, it's
Zanzibar:
smugglers and palm trees, ceiling fans,

sunsets that knock you out like a tropical cocktail.
Pasha, parading
today's

gold favorite on your arm,
how your heart swells
at the blue

view from the old slave fort!
The morning's parasols
bow down before you,

tearing your blood orange
on the café terrace
while upstairs in a closet

old postcards
rave in their box like the sea.
Here is Paris, here Seville, and here

at the back are the chill
polders,
clouds full of tears,

starched curtains hiding pale, furious wives
whose potato-faced couriers
are even now setting out to find you.

What I Understood

When I was a child I understood everything
about, for example, futility. Standing for hours
on the hot asphalt outfield, trudging for balls
I'd ask myself, how many times will I have to perform
this pointless task, and all the others? I knew
about snobbery, too, and cruelty—for children
are snobbish and cruel—and loneliness: in restaurants
the dignity and shame of solitary diners
disabled me, and when my grandmother
screamed at me, "Someday you'll know what it's like!"
I knew she was right, the way I knew
about the single rooms my teachers went home to,
the pictures on the dresser, the hoard of chocolates,
and that there was no God, and that I would die.
All this I understood, no one needed to tell me.
the only thing I didn't understand
was how in a world whose predominant characteristics
are futility, cruelty, loneliness, disappointment
people are saved every day
by a sparrow, a foghorn, a grassblade, a tablecloth.
This year I'll be
thirty-nine, and I still don't understand it.

Evening in the Mugello

The moon lifts in the blue above the blue forest
blank as a zero or a communion wafer.
The children are gone. The dog's grave's lost in the grass.
We plash to the chapel through the ruined garden:
black leaves, dry clatter of rose canes.
The only human sound is Graziano's
television: guns and laughter.
It's old people here, drinking their limoncello.

Seen right, according to Epictetus,
sorrow and joy are the same. But who believes it?
Star without parallax, dark water,
at the last possible moment
we still want to love
whatever it is we've spent our lives loving

as the world creaks on its hinges,
an old house haunted by furniture
settling into itself at the edge of winter.

Always Already

Always already, the word within the world.
So the spider spins the same web each morning
and you are born into meaning

like a serf into a ditch—
this is your horizon:
a huddle of huts, smoke lifting

into a bloody sunset. So
culture is a kind of nature,
a library of oak leaves

muttering their foregone oracles
while stars wheel in their fixed
imaginary constellations

and out in the harbor
a mermaid drowns in the net
from which if a small silver herring should escape

it is only into the greater net, the ocean.

Walking in the Mist

When I was eight or nine, I used to play
that suddenly I'd become invisible.
I'd walk alone down the long school-basement hallway

past the art room, past the big girls' lockers,
the kitchen smelling of bean-steam, tapioca,
the cook's Pall Malls, and tell myself, *All this*

is another dimension, separate from you
till even the scuffed linoleum took on
a radium-dial strangeness, a queer glow—

I had made it happen. No one could see me.
It was like falling off the edge of the world
or coming back again as a ghost to find

everything solid and dense and huge but me.
What did that game mean? Loneliness? A kind
of backward solipsism? Probably

only a silly thrill in scaring myself
that got out of hand: I'd end up panicking
up the stairs in search of anyone who'd

look at me and make me real again.
Walking in mist should be the opposite:
drained of depth and color and perspective

it's trees and stones and thistles that go thin
and sink down into chilly silence. Yet
it doesn't make the difference it should

whether it's you or the world that turns to ghost.
Relation is what matters. When it's broken
it's hard not to suspect that life is just

the clearing you happen to stand in the center of.
No wonder you quicken your steps when you walk in mist
and welcome the sight of even a wrong companion,

a troubled house, so long as it's well lit.

The White Room

Possible to believe in a bearable sort of life
in a white room in one of the tidy anonymous streets
that flash by the elevated subway. Picture it:
a blue chair for reading, a gas ring
for coffee, the lamp in its cheap shade
casting its circle of light. Outside,
soot sifts down on the cornflowers in the vacant lot,
the tailor goes down to the corner for the paper,
the sandwich man stands in his doorway
listening to the Saturday opera on the radio.
You pass and exchange grave nods
with your neighbors, fellow anchorites
proud in your way to have chosen for discipline
a solitude you tell yourself
you probably would have come to anyway.

Trying to Write a Poem Against the War

My daughter, who's as beautiful as the day,
hates politics: *Face it, Ma,*
they don't care what you think! All
passion, like Achilles,
she stalks off to her room,
to confide in her purple guitar and await
life's embassies. She's right,
of course: bombs will be hurled
at ordinary streets
and leaders look grave for the cameras,
and what good are more poems against war
the real subject of which
so often seems to be the poet's superior
moral sensitivities? I could
be mailing myself to the moon
or marrying a pine tree,
and yet what can we do
but offer what we have?
and so I spend
this cold gray milky morning
trying to write a poem against war
that perhaps may please my daughter
who hates politics
and does not care much for poetry, either.

Old

No one left to call me Penelope,
mourned the old countess, on being informed of the death
of her last childhood friend. Did she sit long

in the drafty hall, thinking, That's it then,
nobody left but hangers-on and flunkies,
why go on? Death can't help but look friendly
when all your friends live there, while more and more

each day's like a smoky party
where the music hurts and strangers insist that they know you
till you blink and smile and fade into the wall
and stare at your drink and take a book off the shelf

and close your eyes for a minute and suddenly
everyone you came in with has gone
and people are doing strange things in the corners.
No wonder you look at your watch

and say to no one in particular,
If you don't mind, I think I'll go home now.

Silent Letter

It's what you don't hear
that says struggle
as in wrath and wrack
and wrong and wrench and wrangle.

The noiseless wriggle
of the hooked worm
might be a shiver of pleasure
not a slow writhing

on a scythe from nowhere.
So too the leisure seeming
of a girl alone in her blue
bedroom late at night

who stares at the bitten
end of her pen
wondering how to write
so that what she writes

stays written.

Dreaming About the Dead

You'd think they'd just been out for a casual stroll
and found themselves by chance on the old street,
the old key still in their pocket, the way

they're sitting at the kitchen table when you come in.
Don't you believe it. They've obviously spent hours
arranging for the light to fall with that

phony lambency,
and haven't you noticed how slyly
they look at you when they think you're not looking at them?

True, it seems strange that they would come so far
to warn you against the new girl in the office
or give you a recipe for worms on toast,

but try it, interrupt, say *mirror of ashes,*
moonless heart—they'll only
smile a little vaguely, start hunting for matches,

and suddenly the black car's at the door.
Will you come back? you call out after them.
Oh, definitely, no problem there. Again

and again, until
you learn they will never say what you need them to:
My death was mine. It had nothing to do with you.

Small Comfort

Coffee and cigarettes in a clean café,
forsythia lit like a damp match against
a thundery sky drunk on its own ozone,

the laundry cool and crisp and folded away
again in the lavender closet—too late to find
comfort enough in such small daily moments

of beauty, renewal, calm, too late to imagine
people would rather be happy than suffering
and inflicting suffering. We're near the end,

but O before the end, as the sparrows wing
each night to their secret nests in the elm's
    green dome,
let the last bus bring

lover to lover, let the starveling
dog turn the corner and lope suddenly,
miraculously, down its own street, home.

Wisdom of the Desert Fathers

True, in the legends
they always seemed to be quarreling,
but no one got blood on the sheets
or wept, "You never talk to me! Talk to me!"
The lizards didn't mind the silent treatment

and at first it was exciting, snubbing the tourists
and pretending not to care how the others smelled.
Flash floods and lightning, daybreak
smiting the cliffs like judgment
said KEEP OUT THIS MEANS YOU. Inside,

the caves were plain, but tidy, like motel rooms,
the straw beds tucked each morning with hospital corners,
on the nightstand *Better Mulches,* and a mouse
trained for a year with bread crumbs
to stand and fold its delicate paws in prayer.

Before they knew it, it was too late to go back:
the farm had gone under, cancer had taken Mother,
everyone was married. Even the demons
hardly came round anymore
with their childish bribes of money and sex.

Still, it was years before anyone asked out loud
if the wisdom of the desert fathers
had only been not to be fathers.
Then came the real temptations:
flowering cactus with its dime-store scent

drenching the cool blue twilight,
or the rinsed simple mornings
when it almost seemed they'd wakened
to find themselves back home in the neighborhood:
bachelor uncles, washing the car on Sundays.

Lunaria

Now that I am
All done with spring
Rampant in purple
And ragged leaves

And summer too
Its great green moons
Rising through
The breathless air

Pale dusted like
The luna's wings
I'd like to meet
October's chill

Like the silver moonplant
Honesty
That bears toward winter
Its dark seeds

A paper lantern
Lit within
And shining in
The fallen leaves.

Acknowledgments

Acknowledgment is gratefully made to the following publications, in which these poems first appeared:

The Atlantic: "Mind-Body Problem," "Atlantis," "Maya," "Epithalamion."

Grand Street: "Visitors," "Happiness Writes White."

The Nation: "Trying to Write a Poem Against the War."

The New Republic: "Rereading Jane Austen's Novels," "Night Subway," "From a Notebook," "Walking in the Mist."

The New York Times Book Review: "Forwarding Address."

The New Yorker: "Lives of the Nineteenth-Century Poetesses," "A Walk," "Aere Perennius," "Collectibles," "Signs and Portents," "Shore Road," "Lilacs in September," "Mandarin Oranges," "Playground," "Abandoned Poems," "A Chinese Bowl," "Amor Fati," "Milkweed," "The Expulsion," "Cities of the Plain," "Rapture," "Dreaming About the Dead," "Small Comfort," "Wisdom of the Desert Fathers," "Moth."

Paris Review: "Integer Vitae," "The Heron in the Marsh," "Always Already," "The White Room."

Poetry: "Old Sonnets."

Slate: "Lot's Wife," "In the Bulrushes."

Southwestern Review: "Near Union Square," "The Old Neighbors."

Yale Review: "Two Cats," "What I Understood."

The following poems also appeared in anthologies: "Mind-Body Problem," *The Oxford Book of American Poetry* (Oxford) and *The KGB Bar Book of Poems* (Perennial); "Lives of the Nineteenth-Century Poetesses," *Where Books Fall Open* (Godine); "Mandarin Oranges," *Sustenance and Desire* (Godine); "Playground," *Ecstatic Occasions, Expedient Forms* (Michigan University Press), *Roots & Flowers* (Henry Holt), and *Enduring Ties* (Steerforth Press); "Night Subway," *The Best American Poetry 1991* (Scribner); "The Expulsion," *Letters to the World* (Red Hen Press); "Trying to Write a Poem Against the War," *Poets Against the War* (Nation Books); "Wisdom of the Desert Fathers," *Fatherhood* (Everyman).

KATHA POLLITT is the author of four books of essays and *Antarctic Traveller,* a collection of poems. She has won many prizes and awards for her work, including a National Book Critics Circle Award for Poetry, two National Magazine Awards for essays and criticism, a National Endowment for the Arts grant, a Guggenheim Fellowship, and a Whiting Writer's Fellowship. She writes a column on politics and culture for *The Nation.* She lives in New York City with her husband, Steven Lukes.